A LIFE AS A BLUENOSE

The Story Of An Evertonian

Anthony Hogan

CONTENTS

CHAPTER 1: THE MAKING OF A BLUENOSE

I was nine years old when mum finally gave in and let me attend a football match. My older brother had been a few times even though he was not really interested. Even my sister had been, I mean come on now!! let me go. Dad was a keen Everton fan who travelled everywhere to watch his beloved team. He may have failed to inject the passion into my older siblings, but with me he knew he was on to a winner. I would sit with dad after he returned home from a game and ask him all about it. He would talk me through it and I would listen in awe, fascinated by the events and the players. Dad had already taught me the words to many of the team's songs, and I had been belting them out from an early age. Mum of course worried about me going into the rough and tumble of a football crowd. I begged her, pleaded, sobbed, but her foot was down and I was too small was all she would say. Dad, however, was now on the case, and as this was Everton he would win.

School ended and the summer holidays began. The world cup and the wonderful Dutch team had become a memory. August reared its head and the talk began of the coming new season. Then, I heard those magic words from dad "Everton play tomorrow and you are coming with me" oh!!! the joy. I could hardly sleep and the next morning I was up early and eager. I walked with dad to the shop for his morning paper, I was not planning to leave his side in case mum changed his mind. The morning went so slowly, but just after dinner he said " let's go" and proudly I marched out the door draped in an oversized blue and white scarf, off to my first match.

August 17th 1974, that was the day that I was inducted to the school of bluenoses. I cannot remember how we got to the ground, but it was probably via a few pubs as my dad liked his pint. My arrival; however, I remember in all its glee. It was the crowd that first got to me, and I recall the excitement as me and dad were swept along. I could see nothing as everyone was taller than me, but I caught glimpses of things between people. Blue and white flags and scarves, and policemen. The noise was terrific with people talking and shouting "Get yer Badges, scarves, hats, programmes. The smell in the air was hot-dogs, chip shops, ciggies and stale beer. We came out of the crowd into a clearing, with lines of people who were going into small doors. Dad joined a line and pulled me in front of him "stay by me" he said as we moved along. The line became smaller while the door got bigger, I was almost there. Then, I passed through the door and a blooming great big steel turnstile stopped me. Dad gave some guy behind a cage money and I heard a click, dad pushed the turnstile and we were in.

I think my dad had become an early trendsetter for health and safety as he had taking us into the Park End stand. But Hey!! I was at Goodison. My first impression of it was why did it have so many stairs? They went on forever. Finally, we made it to the top and came out onto the stand. The green of the pitch hit me straight away, as did the size of the crowds. Dad bought me a programme and a bag of sweets and we found our seats. I found it hard to take it all in, and kept looking at all the stands, but I was loving it, and no teams were even out yet.

Finally, a huge roar went up and the team emerged. The noise was amazing as they all sang "Everton,Everton, Everton" I was in heaven. Derby County were the opposition who featured Colin Todd, Archie Gemmill, Bruce Rioch, and fat Franny Lee (my dad called him that) But stuff them, I was here to see Everton. Suddenly the names that dad had told me about were on the pitch in front of me. Colin Harvey, Mick Buckley, Joe Royle, Roger Kenyon, and of course the guy that dad had been raving on about, big Bobby Latchford.

The wonderful sight that is Goodison Park

I would like to tell you that I knew every move that was played and that I could see the chances unfold and the mistakes being made. In reality; however, I had no idea what was going on. Every time the crowd stood up and ooooed and aaarghed, I was convinced that we had scored a goal. In my head it was about 21-0 to us by half time, so I was a bit stunned when dad informed me that it was 0-0? The interval, it still bores me as much today as it did that very first time, it still goes on forever, and I still do not see why players need a break. OK I am being selfish.

At last the second half started. The noise continued, and by the time that I had us 7-0 up, the swearing from those around us began to get worse. Dad looked at me as if to say "don't listen" We never swore, and I had never heard my dad do it, but something told me that he gave it a right good go when he was at a game with his mates. The final whistle blew and everyone stood up and an applause went up. I had us winning that half 18-0, but no! The game had ended goalless.

We made our way back down the thousands of steps again. This time the stairway was jam-packed and dad had a tight hold of my back. Outside we joined the crowds again. The walk was slow, but I did not care. I was still excited about seeing Everton play, plus I was with my dad, just me and him and I loved that. As we walked the crowd became thinner, and soon I had clear room to walk alongside my dad. A lorry beeped and someone shouted my dad's name. It was one of his friends and he told us to jump on the back. On the back? Oh yes. Dad lifted me up and some guy grabbed me and pulled me on. There were loads of people on the back and the driver picked up a few more before heading off. He began to drop people off, mainly outside pubs. Then, it was our turn and we climbed down from the lorry at the end of our road. I had made 70p from dads mates during the ride so I was very happy indeed.

I read every word in my match programme that evening, and it stayed on the table next to my bed when I soundly slept that night. I must have read it thirty times during the following week. It remained my prized possession for many years until my dim-wit of a brother sold it along with my other programmes at a car boot sale. But the memory was still there, and I was now a fully paid up bluenose at last, well my dad had paid really, but you know what I mean.

Derby County went on to win the league that season. So, I had seen the future champions in my first ever game, just the wrong side. Two weeks later dad took me again, and again it was in the Park End Stand. I was left in little doubt that we had scored when I heard the roar for an Everton goal for the very first time. Bob Latchford bagged both goals as we beat Arsenal 2-1. This was followed by another 0-0 against wolves, a 3-2 win versus Leeds, and a 1-1 draw with Newcastle. We beat Man City 2-0, before it was time for my first ever derby match against Liverpool, boo!!!. It was heaving with people at this game and someone had let a load of Liverpool fans in. It was the Street End stand for us as we watched yet another 0-0 game. The noise had been incredible at this match, and the swearing, oh the swearing.

The name sitting proudly on the stadium

On 21st December Carlise United gave me the honour (or not) of witnessing my first every Everton defeat. Four days before Christmas you gits. I hated Carlise for years for that. But nothing could take away my excitement of attending a game, even a defeat. By the end of the season the programme stack in my bedroom had grown to twelve. I still hated evening games as mum refused to allow me to go because of boring school. Dad still brought me home a programme, but I put those in their own pile away from the games I had attended. I also was not allowed to go with dad to any away games, mum had put her foot down on that one. Dad would go to most of them and tell me all about them.

I was happy to have seen twelve games in my first season, in my eyes I was now a regular. The making of me as a bluenose was complete. I was hooked and I craved more. It was three long months until the season started again. It is even longer when you are a kid. In that time I turned 10 and broke up for the school summer holidays. It soon passed and as the new season dawned the excitement was still there, a much as it ever was. This is what I wanted, Come on Everton!!!.

CHAPTER 2: IF YOU KNOW YOUR HISTORY

History; one of the few things at school that I was actually interested in. I have always been fascinated by the past, none more so than my family history. Funny enough I was able to trace my family support of Everton football club back to at least 1906 through a family story. My great grandma Sarah was a very religious lady, though she liked the odd tipple. She could sometimes be found in one of the public houses close to St Anthony's church on Scotland Road, where after a few drinks, she was know to burst into song. One of her favourite songs after a drinking was to sing the line "Sandy scored the goal". This was in reference to Alex 'Sandy' Young, who scored Everton's winning goal in the 1906 FA cup final against Newcastle United. Sarah was aged 30 in 1906, so the cup final win must have been a big thing in the city as it certainly left its mark on her. It is nice to know that football was so important to people in those days.

My grandfather was an Everton fan who went to watch their home games. He would have witnessed the great Dixie Dean playing. Sadly he never had the opportunity to take his little boy (my father) to an Everton match. Grandfather fought during WW2 as a gunner with the Royal Artillery. Leaving the UK in late 1940, he spent three years defending Malta before moving into Italy. He never received any leave during his time at war. So, after 1940 my dad never saw him again as he was killed while fighting in early 1944. In a well-tended cemetery in Italy rests not only a war hero, but a fellow bluenose.

My dad wanted to go and see Everton play as soon as he could, and he first went when he was a lot blooming younger than I was!! It was his uncle Richard who first took him along to a match. His mum and her older brother were both Liverpool fans, but thankfully her younger brother Richard had seen sense. I can also trace a Liverpool supporters line in my family back to the 1920s, but lets not mention that in case I get stick for it. My dad's uncle Austin had tried to get him to go and watch Liverpool, but dad was having none of it and refused to go, well in dad.

So, dad had earned his bluenose stripes and started going to all the home games. He was crazy about Everton, so much so that when his mother remarried in 1948 he went to the match instead of the wedding. After he had left school and started working, he had the money to follow the team to away games. Dad was also a very good footballer. He played as a striker and once scored nine goals in one game. Dad was spotted by talent scouts, but had only one team that he wanted to play for, Everton. He turned down all the offers he received from other clubs and waited for the toffee's, they soon came calling. Everton's attention had been drawn towards my dad, and after his trial with the club he signed a contract to say he would return to them after he had finished his army national service.

Dad was now in the Royal Artillery and was sent out to Hong Kong. The army had spotted his footballing talents and decided that he was best suited to them by playing exhibition matches. Dad agreed, and was soon the star man in the team. During one game he injured his knee and had to rest it. The army were keen for him to get back playing and offered him painkilling injections that would help him play. In hindsight it was a stupid decision by dad to accept the treatment, but he was a 19 year old lad who loved playing football. Dad later found out that the army doctor had been pumping cortisone into his knee.

On his return to the UK he was seen by a doctor who told him he needed to rest his knee and not to play any football for a few months. Dad was then sent out to Germany to finish his service. Here, he found himself under pressure from the top brass who wanted to show off their star striker. He agreed to play and again he took the injections. For months he played on, game after game, until his injury forced him to be rested. After his service was over, he returned home and attended a meeting with Everton. The club told him straight away that his knee was never going to be strong enough for him to play at the top level. It was all over for him, he was never going to play for his beloved Everton.

Old turnstiles stored in the ground

Dad carried on playing Sunday league football, where even with a dodgy knee he was a cut above most of the other players. After a couple of years his knee became troublesome, and he was forced to give up the game that he loved so much at a young age. Nobody can tell what the outcome would have been if my dad had not played football for the army or taken those injections. He may have been a flop as a top level footballer, but then again? None of that matters now as it was not to be for him. Later when I was doing my athletics training he did say to me "If a doctor ever offers you cortisone, punch the bastard in the face". That was the only time that I ever saw him angry about what had happened to him, but I guess it really did upset him at the time.

I had made my entrance on the world in 1965, and dad quickly had me named after an Everton player. Tony Kay was the guy chosen as my namesake, yes!!, I was named after someone who received a lifetime ban. Kay had been banned after placing a bet on his team Sheffield Wednesday, to lose against Ipswich Town in 1962. A few weeks after this game he was transferred to Everton and became part of their title winning side. In 1964 the story of the betting scandal hit the papers and resulted in a court case. Kay was implicated and in January of 1965 he was sentenced to four months imprisonment. On his release he was banned from playing football for life. Yes he did wrong, but that ban was very harsh and robbed us of a great talent. Kay would no doubt have been a part of England's 1966 world cup squad. He later played charity matches alongside local musicians for the Merseybeat Eleven team, playing alongside another of my idols Rory Storm. I am proud and honoured to be named after such a great footballer.

My dad remained a huge Everton fan and followed them home and away. In 1963 he saw them crowned league champions, and then it was on to 1966. That was the year that dad always liked to talk about, but with so much happening that year who can blame him. Everton went on a run in the FA cup that took them to the semi finals and a tie against Manchester United at Bolton's Burnden Park stadium. Dad went to the match on his own. With just over ten minutes of the game remaining, Colin Harvey struck his shot into the united net to make it 1-0 to the blues. As the fans celebrated someone jumped on my dad's back cheering. When he finally broke free dad discovered that the guy on his back was his uncle Richard, neither of them had realised that the other was at the match. Everton had made it to the cup final, dad was going to Wembley.

Dad was going to be at the final, there was no doubt about that, but he had a problem, his job. He worked Saturday mornings, and getting the time off would be difficult for him. In the end dad threw a sickie and set off on the coach for Wembley. Along the way they made a stop so everyone could have a break, stretch of the legs, cup of tea etc. As they climbed off the coach a guy from a newspaper asked them if he could take a photograph of them all. They were happy to do it and all lined up to pose for the pic. After a short break it was back aboard, and onwards to Wembley.

Everton had become the first team to reach an FA cup final without conceding a goal. However, after 57 minutes they found themselves 2-0 down as Sheffield Wednesday brushed them aside. Everton looked down and out, but their response was immediate and clinical. What followed was one of the greatest Cup final fight backs ever to be witnessed as Mike Trebilcock knocked in two quick goals to bring the score level. With sixteen minutes remaining of the game Derek Temple latched on to a mistake, before slotting the ball past Ron Springett in the Wednesday goal. Everton had snatched the victory. Dad made it onto the pitch as the team celebrated with the cup and managed to dig himself up a bit of turf that he brought back with him and placed in the flower box outside our front door.

Dad returned home on the coach, probably drunk, but certainly delighted. On Monday morning when he arrived at work he was told that the boss wanted a word with him in the office. Dad went in to see him and the boss asked him if he was feeling better after being off sick on Saturday. Dad told him he was much better before the boss put a newspaper in front of him that had the photo of him and his mates posing for the newspaper guy on the way to Wembley. Dad was stunned, and as his boss was a reds fan he feared the worst. His boss, however, burst out laughing and told him that he only needed to ask and he would have been given the time off. He then congratulated dad on his team's victory and sent him back to work ... Phew!!!!

1966 was a great time for any football fan in the Merseyside area. Everton had won the cup and Liverpool the league. Now, the world cup arrived on our doorstep with a number of games being played at Goodison Park. I was still in my nappies so I remember nothing about it all. However, dad would relay the stories of when he saw mighty Brazil and the brilliant Pele and Eusabio grace the Everton turf. Telling me how Brazil were knocked out and of how great Portugal played. He also talked about one of the greatest games that he ever witnessed, Portugal against the not so mighty North Korea. The Koreans had stunned the football world by beating Italy 1-0 and qualifying from their group. Now they faced Portugal and at Goodison Park in what was surely just a formality for Eusabio and his boys. I listened in thrilled silence as dad talked about the shock that ran throughout the crowd as the Koreans scored. Then, it was 2-0, and after half an hour 3-0. A dazed Portugal managed to get themselves together and fought back to win 5-3, but it was the Koreans who received the applause of the crowd that day.

One day a council worker turned up at our house to paint the outside. He was to paint the window frames and front door as well as the wood on the canopy. The canopy wood hung down in small spiked slats and these were to be painted red and white. The front door was to be painted red, oh dear! Enter dad. He told the worker he did not have to paint it, but the man explained that he had too as his boss would check. Dad told him to go ahead then and the man got on with the job. Later that day a man in a suit arrived and spoke to the workman. Dad came out and asked him if he was the guys boss, and when he replied "Yes" my dad said "OK" and went into the house. He came out with a tin of royal blue gloss paint and said to the guy "See that, your man has painted it red and done his job". With that dad opened his tin and started to paint over all the red bits. We had the only blue and white canopy in the area.

These signs are sprayed all over the ground

Alan Ball, joined Everton soon after he had been victorious with England when winning the world cup. Ball was certainly one of the greatest midfielders to ever grace a football pitch. Simply, he was world class and seemed to be able to run forever. He teamed up with Howard Kendall and Colin Harvey to form one of the best midfield partnerships that Everton have ever produced. The trio were given the nickname of 'The Holy Trinity' and it was said that they could find each other in the dark.

My dad raved about these three players, but to be fair, he also told me never to forget the other guys that played in the fantastic Everton team of the next few years. In 1968 Everton and dad were back at Wembley, this time losing out by the single goal to West Bromwich Albion. Two years later the blues were League champions again with probably one of the best Everton teams ever to have been assembled.

I once asked dad who was the best player he had ever seen play. I waited in anticipation to hear the name of an Everton legend. Without hesitation dad replied "Duncan Edwards", What? I then asked "What about the great Everton players? or Pele? Or Eusabio?", but again he said "Duncan Edwards" I must admit I was a bit stunned by this, but dad explained "You asked who was the best, and in my opinion Duncan was. He could do anything and play anywhere. I cried when I heard he had died". I was by now astounded. How could dad say that a Man Utd player was the best he had seen? He went on "Never wish injury on any player as they are playing the game that we love. Enjoy their talents even if they are not from your own team". Dad taught me a valuable lesson that day. I still do not like seeing players out injured, and I have admired many opposition players over the years, even if they did run riot over Everton.

Dad continued to watch Everton, all home games and many away. He failed to get my older brother to more than two games as he just was not interested. My sister attended a few before she became bored with going. Later in life she would meet a guy who supported Liverpool and she followed them!! You traitor sis!!. We moved house and the wembley turf in the plant pot came with us, being laid in the back garden of our new home. Then, it was my turn to go to see Everton play, and I was hooked. And, that brings us back up to 1975.

CHAPTER 3: THE STREET END BECKONS

August 1975, and at long last the season was back. Off I went with dad to see Everton's opening game, full of hope and excitement. We got thumped 4-1 by Coventry. Losing could not put me off and we were soon back to winning ways. I just loved to attend a football match, I enjoyed everything. Even if we lost it was a great day out to me.

As the season went on I started to have my favourite players. Bob Latchford was my top player, but I also held Mick Lyons and Martin Dobson in high esteem. By the following season, Andy King and Duncan McKenzie had been added to my list. Dad was still taking me into the stands to watch the games. I would sit there looking at the Gwladys Street End as it always amazed me. So many people where in there, they swayed and made so much noise. That is where all the songs started from, and that is where I wanted to be. I did ask dad if we could go in there, but he would just say "When you are older". Bah! Sugar lumps.

After one game, I had asked dad if I could have a hot-dog from the stall by the entrance to Stanley Park. He replied " Where do you think he goes for a wee?". I looked around and assumed he went in the bushes. "Yes" said dad " and where does he wash his hands?". Uuuurgh!!!! Dad must have seen the look of horror on my face as he then asked "do you want a hot-dog then?" I most certainly did not and we got chips from a shop as we walked along. I have never ever wanted a hot-dog from that day to this.

I was still under mums ban of no evening or away matches, though I was going to almost every home game on a Saturday afternoon. Everton then went on a run in the league cup, reaching the semi-final before Christmas of 1976. Not that I got to see any of the games with my evening match ban. I did, however, make it to my first ever FA cup fixture just after the new year, where I watched the mighty blues beat Stoke City 2-0. Within weeks Everton had not only progressed to the 6th round of the FA cup, but had beaten Bolton Wanders to make it to the final of the League cup. Everton were at Wembley and mum said "Not a chance you are going" Waaah!!!! My excitement was still going through the roof. At last I had a chance to see my team lift a trophy. They had won things when I was a baby and a toddler, but this was my first real chance to see it myself.

March of 1977 saw my utter brilliant Everton (Hooray) take on Aston Villa (Boo! Hiss! Boooo!!) The nerves had come and were no better after league cup final ended 0-0 after a very boring game. A replay was needed the following Wednesday at Hillsborough. This game finished 1-1 after extra-time and a second replay was needed. When would they be able to fit it in and play it? I will tell you shall I, four bloody weeks later. Yes four more stupid, long, dragging weeks to see if we would win the cup. In the meantime we had the small matter of a FA cup quarter final and a local derby. I tell you, it was a terrible time for the nerves. I was there to see us sail past Derby County to reach another Semi-final, but mum banned me from the mid-week local derby that once again ended up 0-0. I saw us stuff Spurs and lose to Man Utd. Then, it was time for the league cup final, again.

For any younger readers, let me explain something. Back in 1977 there was no TV coverage of the league cup final. You went the game or you listened on a radio. I had to tune in the radio and follow the commentary. The game would be settled that evening, by penalties if needed. It finished 2-2 after ninety minutes. Extra-time came and had almost passed. Penalties where coming as there was little time left to play. And, then, a mistake from a Villa cross let in Brian bloody Little to tap in the winner. I was gutted and sick as a pig, heartbroken even. I wanted them to start the game again, I wanted my trophy. I was only 11.

While on the subject of radio coverage back in those days, let me explain how techno it all was. Well..erm.., it wasn't. In fact, it was pretty bad, with just the second half being covered. You would still tune in at the start even though they played records and went to the game about every fifteen minutes for an update. If one of the local teams was losing at half-time our radio station would play a Beatles song to try and help them to score. When you look back now it all seems a bit nuts, but this was top excitement back then. I can remember games when Everton were losing and I would be screaming at the radio "play a Beatles song". Ha ha, good times.

The final had made me feel cheated out of a trophy, but that was nothing to what was coming next. Ten days later Everton played their local rivals Liverpool in the FA cup semi-final at Maine Road in Manchester. It was a thrilling game that had everything. Everton twice came from behind and as the game neared its end the score stood at 2-2. Then, Ronny Goodlass picked up the ball and drove down the wing before sending in cross that Bryan Hamilton turned into the Liverpool net. The Evertonians went crazy, the Everton players celebrate, while the Liverpool players sank in despair. Everton had done it and were on their way to Wembley .. Oh hang on! I forgot about Clive fucking Thomas. Clive, that bad meth of a ref, decided it was not a goal. No flag had gone up and no clear explanation was ever given as to why he disallowed it? But he did, and Everton had had their place in the final ripped away from them. It was another sickening kick in the teeth for us, but this one stunk of a cheating referee.

Four days later we lost the replay and my dream of seeing us win a trophy was over. The next day at school I was introduced to another Merseyside footballing must, the banter. The red kids were waiting for us blues with their "your crap, poo, plop" (I have kept it clean). It went on for most of the day, but it never bothered me. I liked it and I still do as long as it remains fun and does not turn into vicious hatred as it can often do. The season had ended like a damp squid, but I would be back for more come August.

The new season began with a defeat to Nottingham Forest. I had another favourite player to add to my list in the shape of Dave Thomas, who sprinted the wings in his rolled down socks. I also had a new Everton Ally in the shape of a lad named Marty who had joined our school before the summer holidays had started. His family had moved into a house not far from mine, and being both nuts on Everton we soon became friends. Marty came with an added bonus, his family. They all attended the Everton games, his parents, brothers and his sister. Dad agreed that I could start going to games with Marty and I was over the moon. Not that I was bored of going with my dad, it was just a mates thing, and I wanted to get into the Street End.

September 3rd 1977. That was the day that I finally made it into the Gwladys Street end of the ground. Myself and Marty had met up and travelled to the ground by bus. We had to change buses and jump aboard a number 27. I can still recall how you used to have to pay the correct money on this bus. Along the way it would pick up a number of blues as well as some of those reds fans. They were heading off to the reserve game at Anfield and we would call them part-time supporters as they all got off. Being two silly young kids we would hold our breath when the bus stopped next to the kop, or shout out loud "What's that smell, it stinks" once the bus moved on we would shout "Thank god, I can get some fresh air now". Two stops later we would jump off and walk down Sleepers Hill and into Stanley Park. The walk through the park takes about five to ten minutes, but we would take around half an hour as we climbed on the lake bridges or threw stones into the water. Then, we would come out and there it was. That wonderful old bitch that is Goodison.

The closet I could get to taking a photo from my spec as a kid

 On that first day at a game with Marty, we headed for the Gwladys Street and took our place first in line. It was only about 12:45 pm, but we were so excited about going in there that we wanted to get in first. As the crowd and the line got bigger we held on to those turnstile doors and defended them with our lives. Well, that is how us two kids saw it anyway. At last we heard that magic click and the doors slid open. In we went, paid our money, and ran up the steps. We stopped in awe as we saw the pitch. We were there at last, standing on the Street End. Of course it was deserted as it was still ninety minutes to kick off. But nothing could take away the excitement and pride that we felt about being there.

Marty's older brother had told us about a spot in the corner near the Bullens Road that was just above the middle walkway. He told us to stand behind the front bar and he would meet us there later. Sure enough he turned up and found us, telling us what a great view it was from here. About twenty minutes from kick-off, Marty and his brother started waving at the crowd to our left. Looking across I spotted their parents and sister sitting in the Lower Bullens. It turned out that they were season tickets holders and our spec in the ground was one where they could keep an eye on us. It was a great view from there though.

The crowd started to get bigger and the spaces around us began to fill. You could feel the buzz among the spectators all waiting in anticipation for the game to start. Then, it came, those wonderful first notes of 'Z Cars'. The crowd erupted into cheers and applause for their heroes, who ran out of the tunnel and straight towards the Street End goal. The noise was ear-splitting, and much more louder than I had heard from the stands, and the atmosphere was electric. The crowd sang as one and I joined in with them, it was magic, pure magic.

I was now seeing the players and the action close up. The crowd around me reacted to every chance on goal with jumping, pushing and deafening cheers. I watched as those in the middle swayed forward. I wanted a be a part of that, but for today I was happy to watch from where I stood. Wolves were our opponents that day and the game finished 0-0 (I am seeing a pattern here) but nothing could tarnish the thrill that I had gained from standing on the Street End. Well, almost nothing. As we headed back through Stanley Park we saw the lines of buses that were picking up the Wolves fans. Then, some idiot threw something at one of the buses and a window shattered. These buses were filled to the brim with fans and I stood there in shock wondering if the people behind the window were OK? I was fuming that some low life had done something as stupid as that. I was the kid here, disgusted by the actions of some pathetic coward of an adult. I never told dad about this incident in case he insisted on taking me to the match.

I still attended games with Marty. Mostly in the same spec in the Street End, but not always. Marty wanted to try out other areas of the ground so we sometimes went in elsewhere. After a few games, we had teamed up with three other lads who like us were early arriver's at the stadium. We had our own gang and it was fun. We would all giggle at some of the things that got shouted during a game, and became good match buddies together. For one match we all decided, for some reason, to go into the Street End stand. Our seats were near the back and we went down to the front before the game to look over the pitch. One of the lads was called John, and he had bought himself a fishcake from the chippy outside before we came in. He ate it as we all looked over the front barrier of the stand. Then, his fishcake fell from his paper and dropped down into the Gwladys Street terrace. We all looked over, and there stood a guy looking back at us with bits of fishcake all over his head. Everyone around him was laughing and we all fell about in fits as well. The guy was shouting up that he was going to fucking kill us and this made everyone laugh more. Everyone except John. I can still see his worried face as he shouted down "I never meant it mister". He then ran up to his seat and stayed there all through the game. Terrified that fishcake man was going to come up and get him. He was so scared that the guy was waiting for him outside that we agreed to wait with him until everyone had gone and they asked us to leave. John was fine as there was no sign of any fishcakes outside.

Another mate of ours did not like swearing and cringed whenever the crowd took it up. If a decision went against us the fans would burst into "You're a bastard referee". Our mate, however, had his own version and sang the words "How's your father, How's your father, how's your father referee". That still tickles me to this day. I never got a sweet from the Toffee Lady either as I was too far back in the crowd. But I did hear a number of blokes shouting out to her something about showing them her T .... never mind.

Sadly, as well as the fun, I also witnessed some bad things at the match. The worst was at one game when me, Marty and the other lads were in our spec in the corner of the Gwladys street. A man somewhere behind was screaming all kinds of insults to the oppositions players. One of our gang was a black lad named Paul. He was a great lad, and very funny. I liked him a lot. The man behind began shouting racist insults. I could see Paul starting to get upset by all of this, and it only got worse. Paul burst out crying and jumped down from our spot before running off through an entrance to the back of the stand. One of the lads chased after him to check on him. I was fuming, really angry. How dare this disgusting man upset my friend. I looked back through the crowd and saw him still shouting his abuse. My anger got the better of me and I shouted at him to shut the fuck up. He looked in my direction and told me to "fuck off you little prick". Not put off I screamed back at him "You bully upsetting my mate, you stupid fat fucker". Well, everyone around me burst into laughter and the fat boy racist got a cob on. He did not like it when the abuse and laughter was on him, and the next thing he was heading towards me telling me he was going to fucking dig me one. That is until some guy grabbed him by the throat and told him that if he laid a finger on me he would kick his head in. The racist slid off into the crowd after that.

Our mate came back, but Paul was not with him. He explained that Paul was crying a lot and one of the stewards was trying to calm him down. But he had had enough of hearing those horrible racist insults and wanted to leave the ground. We were all gutted, and if fat boy would have shown his face again I would have gladly kicked him in his ollies. We never saw Paul again. For months we searched for him at every game, but he was never there. I still feel sick in my stomach when I think how a grown man ruined the football experience of a young lad with his horrible remarks. Paul was a decent lad, he never deserved that, but then again, nobody does.

Looking down the Bullens Road

I remember collecting badges that I bought from a stall holder outside the ground. Some were rather funny, but one shocked me, even at such a young age. It read "Bob Latchford Strikes Faster Than The Ripper" in relation to the Yorkshire Ripper who had murdered a number of woman and who was still at large. It stunned and sickened me to read that badge. Many grown men could be seen wearing the badge and I would wonder how they could find it funny. It still worries me now that that badge was ever made.

The games continued with Marty coming along with me. On New Years eve we played Arsenal. The ground was packed full.

Myself and Marty decided that today was the day that we braved standing in the middle of the Street End. I suppose one reason we did it was because it was freezing cold and we would be warmer in there. It was complete mayhem in the middle. The noise was beyond anything we had heard before. I am sure that for one five minute period that my feet did not touch the floor. We got pushed, our feet were stood on, and we would go move six-feet when the crowd lunged forward in anticipation of a goal. We felt hands grabbing us to stop us falling, and giggled to each other when we nearly fell. We loved it, and wondered what it would be like if we actually scored a goal. Well,we did not have long to wait, as Big Bob Latchford gave us the lead early in the game. I never saw the goal, but I was left in no doubt we had scored when I moved about ten feet to the right, felt so many pats on my head and back that I lost count of them, and heard a roar so loud that it seemed everyone was screaming into my ear. At one point during all this madness all I could see was people's legs, so I guess I was almost on the floor? The hands kept hold of me and soon I was up straight again and hugging Marty in celebration. The crowd burst into song "Everton! Everton! Everton!", "By far the greatest team the world has ever seen", " Bobby Latchford walks on water","We love you Everton oh yes we do", "Kopites are gob..." well that is enough of that!! Andy King scored late in the game and we did it all again. Two very happy and thrilled 12 year olds walked through Stanley Park after the game, bought their chips, and jumped on a bus. They told everyone they met that they had been in the middle of the Street End, as if it was going to impress the listener. It had impressed those two lads who went home very happy that day. It is a wonderful memory that I still fondly look back on many times. While it had been great fun in the middle, we returned to our usual space for the next game, we could see the game from there.

In January of 78 we watched Everton beat Aston Villa twice in a week. 4-1 in the FA cup where I think our future striker Andy

Gray scored for Villa? Then, the following week we did them 1-0 in the league. We were also in for a great end to the season. Not a trophy, but to us two young kids, the next best thing. The Daily Express newspaper had offered £10,000 to any player who could score thirty league goals in a season. Our big Bob Latchford was scoring for fun and as the season came to its conclusion he was nearing the target. A penalty in the 1-0 win over Ipswich Town had brought Bob up to 28 goals with three games remaining. However, he failed to score in the following two matches, this left him needing to score two in the final fixture of the season against Chelsea.

Saturday 29th April. Myself and Marty headed off to the ground full of excitement, could Bob do it? To us it like reliving the stories we had heard about the great Dixie Dean scoring 60 goals in a season. For some strange reason, I have no idea why, we chose to go into the Park End terrace that day. However, by the end of the day we would be somewhere else. There were hardly any kids in the Park End, probably as it was a third full of Chelsea fans who had a reputation for violence. We could hear all the abuse flying around from both sets of fans, and curiosity took over us. We edged through the crowd towards the Chelsea fans to see what was going on, and then it all kicked off.

We were caught up in the wave of aggression as both sets of supports turned on each other. One side would run to attack before the other did it back. There was no way out of it. We were stuck and had nowhere to go. At one point the Chelsea fans got within yards of us and I have no shame in admitting that I was terrified. Then, me and Marty felt each other being pulled backwards away from the trouble. We were dragged for about twenty feet before we stopped. Looking behind us we saw a great big bloke who had taken it up himself to get us both away from the fighting. He never said a word to us. He just dragged us some more down to the front where he called over a policeman and said "Get rid of these two will you lad". With the help of the guy and the policeman we were lifted over the wall and onto the track behind the goal. I was hoping that my dad was not watching me in case he went nuts. We were then marched to the Paddock and put in there. We were disgusted as we wanted to go in the Street End.

The game had started and Everton were soon 2-0 up, but no goal for Bobby. Just after half time it was 3-0, but still nothing from Bob. "Come on Bobby" was all you could hear everyone shouting, but time was running out. Then, on 72 minutes, Bob rose to head home, and the ground went crazy. Three minutes later and Mick Lyon's was in. He could shoot, or pass to Bob who was unmarked. Lyon's shot, and made it 5-0. That is the only time I have ever heard the fans groan for an Everton goal. "you greedy sod" I thought as I fumed about Lyon's not laying it on to Bob. Another three minutes passed and Lyon's went down in the box and the ref pointed to the spot. I am still convinced that he dived, but who cares, Bob had his chance. You could feel the tension and expectation from the crowd as Bob laid the ball on the penalty spot. "Come on Bob" I screamed along with the rest of the stadium. As cool as you like Bob slotted the ball home for his 30th league goal. The ground erupted into a frenzy. I am still convinced that the noise generated from that goal gave me the damage to my left ear that I have today.

The last ten minutes or so of the game was just pure singing and happiness. Bob had done it, and we all loved him. The final whistle blew and with it began the charge for the pitch. The stewards just moved aside as the crowd poured on from all directions. Myself and Marty had made it on in a flash. Our first pitch invasion. In the few seconds that it took me to climb over the wall and onto the pitch I thought about my dad at Wembley in 66. With all the chaos going on around me I thumped my heel into the ground a few times and ended up with piece of turf about a foot long. I put it inside my jacket and began to celebrate with the others. When they finally cleared us off the field we jumped into the Street End. So, we managed to make it into three parts of the ground that day. Dad laughed when I showed him the turf back at home. He planted it next to his bit from Wembley.

On our way home from the match that day we jumped aboard a bus and sat at the back. Sitting there were a number of people who were Chelsea fans. They asked us if the bus went into the city centre as they were staying at a hotel there. We told them that it did and started chatting with them. One of the ladies told us she was the mother of the Chelsea player Ray Wilkins. We laughed and said "Oh Yeah!". She told us that she really was and showed us photos of her with him. Before we got off the bus she had given us £1 each. Not a bad sum for a twelve-year old back then. So, the season was over, and although we had won nothing it had been a fantastic ending. One of those days you are proud to say "I was there".

CHAPTER 4: THE TEENAGE YEARS

Before the new season had begun I had turned into a teenager. Yes, I now had an attitude and I knew everything. My teenage years as an Everton fan would produce a mixture of high and lows, but would I ever see my team lift a trophy? The season had started with a win at Chelsea. Now it was time for my first evening fixture that resulted in a victory against Derby. We then won at home to Arsenal before another evening fixture in the league cup against lower league Wimbledon.

We went in the Park End for this fixture. I can remember in the warm up that they put a large football in the centre circle that fell apart and dropped out thousands of packets of crisp. People came around throwing them into the crowd and we got plenty of packets between us. The game itself was a cracker and we gave Wimbledon a thumping. 8-0 we won with Latchford scoring five and Dobson three. We went home singing our heads off. As we passed couple, the guy asked us what was the score. When we told him he started dancing with us. His wife said "he will be dancing in bed tonight".

We had also qualified for the UEFA cup. It was all a knock-out tournament back then, none of this league rubbish that they have now. Our first game was against the Irish team Finn Harps. We won the first leg away 5-0, then beat them at home by the same score. 10-0 on aggregate, wow!! I was sure we would win the cup after a storming victory like that. However, next up was Dukla Prague who knocked us out on the away goal rule. In between that tie we had played the derby match against Liverpool at home. A day I will never forget.

Saturday October 28th. There I was first in line at the Gwladys Street turnstile door clutching my ticket. The crowd was getting big way before usual. People were asking if anyone had any spare tickets for sale. Everyone wanted to get in for the game and some were prepared to go to extreme lengths. A crowd had gathered around a door further along from me. The next thing we heard a commotion and looked across. They had somehow managed to get the door open and were climbing through over the turnstile. A few of them managed to get inside before the police arrived and blocked off the route. When my turnstile opened I was first in and headed for my spot in the corner. I then heard a voice. Looking up I saw a guy above me in the rafters."Any coppers there mate" he asked. I looked and told him none were about and he climbed down saying "Cheers mate".

By the time that the game started the crowd was full to the brim. It was fantastic and the banter flying between the two sets of supports was wonderful. Next to me was a guy in a blue scarf who had sat his little boy, who was wearing a red scarf, on the steel barrier. I just love the way we are in this city over our football. From what I can remember the game was pretty good with chances for both sides. It was 0-0 when the teams went in for the half time break. It may be old age, but I am sure that they held a dog show during the break? One dog jumped through a hoop that was on fire. After it had jumped, a guy went to put the fire out and knocked the stand over onto the turf. There was a burn mark on the pitch for weeks from where it had fallen.

The second half began and the blues were getting stuck in. In the 58th minute we attacked up the left hand side. The ball came back out of the Liverpool box towards Andy King who hit it, oh! How he hit it. I had a fantastic view as the ball flew past Ray Clemence and into the goal. Then, the celebration started with a deafening noise that seemed to go on forever. The place had gone mental. The game restarted and the crowd burst into song. I had never witnessed and atmosphere like it. I think it was David Johnson who almost ruined our day when he poked the ball into our net, but thankfully it was disallowed. With minutes to go I saw the little lad in the red scarf crying and heard his dad say to him "It's OK, you will still win the league". I felt so sorry for him, but Everton had to win. And, they did. It was an amazing feeling to see us beat the old enemy and I travelled home a very happy chappy. A number of reds fans boarded the bus and the banter started. There was nothing nasty about it, and fair play to those reds as they took it all well. That evening I stayed at my Nan's house and watched the game again on Match of the day. My Uncle came home well and truly drunk singing his head of. We went outside to get him in and he picked me up before he tripped and sent us both over the garden fence.

At one game we thought we would try standing behind the goal. They had crates that you could stand upon to see. It was not that good there, but it did produce a very funny moment. Our keeper at the time was Georgie Wood. He was a good shop stopper, but was dodgy with anything coming in from long range. A shot came in and he fluffed at it and just managed to get it around the post for a corner. The crowd was fuming and as Georgie stood against his post for the corner one guy shouted out "Why don't you fuck off Georgie". Another guy replied "Why don't you fuck off" before Georgie shouted "Why don't you all fuck off". This was greeting with laughter and a song for Georgie from the crowd.

By January we were out of all the cups and I was rather miffed by that. The crowds started to fall a bit as well. In February I stood freezing in the Street End with drops dripping from my nose. It was so cold that I was shivering, but it was worth it as we won 4-1 and Andy King bagged a hat-trick. The things we suffer to watch out team. The season carried on, another one without silverware. We finished 4th and I was still confident that we could make a challenge the following season for that elusive trophy.

St Luke's church as much a part of our ground as anything

The new season started with a 4-2 loss to John Bond's Norwich at Goodison. The ground was not as full as it usually was for an opening day fixture, and when we played our next home match against Cardiff it was very bare with gaps everywhere. The midfielder Asa Hartford had signed for Nottingham Forest during the summer, but he was quickly transferred to Everton. On Saturday 1st September he was to make his debut at home to Aston Villa. Myself and Marty were going along to get a good look at him. What followed stunned us both.

We had gone to the game along our usual route. Sitting on the 27 bus, booing as it passed Anfield, then jumping off two stops later. We bought chips from a shop nearby and began our walk down sleepers hill towards Stanley Park. As we strolled a car pulled and a guy shouted "Where is Goodison Park?". Marty was pointing towards the ground and was telling the guy the direction. As he did I looked at the man again "Its Asa Hartford" I shouted". Marty realised it was and we both became star-struck. Asa asked told us that he would give us a lift if we showed him the way. We could have said "It's just over there" but this was a chance not to be missed. There we were, both sitting on the passenger seat next to our new signing, holding our chips. Asa asked for a chip, in fact he had several. We got his autograph on that chip paper as well. Asa told us that he had become lost and driven into Anfield by mistake. He said that the security guard there had laughed at him and said "You are better off staying here mate". Then, we were at the ground and outside the player's entrance, we were only blooming going to drive in. Two very chuffed lads and an Everton footballer drove into the player's car park, my excitement had now gone through the roof. Asa thanked us as he parked and told us to wait with him as he was going to get us some free tickets. We climbed out of the car feeling like stars with all the eyes on us, then the mob arrived. Asa was engulfed by autograph hunters and security arrived to pull people away. They pulled me and Marty away, the stupid gits, we were Asa's mates. Our last view of Asa was seeing him going into the ground frantically looking around. He was clearly searching for us.

Not put off by that stupid security guard we made our way to the Street End. We cheered like mad for Asa during the game and he was now up there in our favourite player list. During and after the game we told everyone the story of how we had been in the car with Asa. Nobody believed us. We were called Billy liars!! and, our mates laughed at us. However, the next day the story appeared in one of the Sunday newspapers. We were not named, but Asa thanked us and even mentioned our chips. We became celebrities at school for the next week. Asa was a real nice guy and left me with a great memory of meeting one of the Everton players.

The Dutch team Feyenoord were our opposition in the first round of the EUFA cup. We lost the first game away 1-0 before they came to Goodison. This was the first game that I swapped my scarf with an away supporter. A Dutch guy beckoned us over outside the ground and offered the swap. I gladly took him up on it and kept the scarf as a memento. Others would come my way over the years, but like my first programme, my stupid brother sold them all at a car boot sale. The game was a nervous one as we tried to level the tie. Fifteen minutes before the end Feyenoord scored, leaving us to find three to win. Bah!! another trophy went astray.

March 1st 1980 was derby day. Liverpool were 2-0 up after half an hour. We had a better second half a pulled a goal back, but the reds held on to beat us. Geoff Nulty had his career ended in this game when Jimmy Case produced one of the most horrific tackles that I have ever witnessed. After the game, we walked along Goodison Road and noticed an ambulance was parked there with people crowded around it. On we went and bought chips before heading for the bus. Arriving home I heard the news that Dixie Dean had died. Dixie had been at the game where he suffered a heart attack. The ambulance that we had passed had been for him. I can still recall the number of Liverpool fans who paid tribute to him in the following weeks. That was a nice touch and showed how highly regarded Dixie was. He was after all a true phenomenon.

Things just got worse. We were very poor in the league that season and hovered around the relegation area. We did have a cup run all the way to the semi-finals, where we lost a replay to West Ham. We ended the season just one place above the relegated teams. It had been awful to watch us perform so badly and to hear the boos ringing out. But this way my team and I would be back for more.

The new season was not much better than the last. Big Bob Latchford hardly played, but we had a decent goalscorer in Peter

Eastoe. John Bailey, Garry Stanley and Kevin Ratcliffe had become regulars, while a striker called Graeme Sharp had made a couple of appearances. We were out of the league cup early, and our league form was not much better than the season before. The FA cup offered the only chance of me finally seeing some glitter being lifted by my team. The draw was unkind to us and threw us in against Arsenal. With minutes to go in the tie it was still 0-0. Then, Kenny Samson put the ball in his own net and we had the lead. Mick Lyons made it two right at the end and we were through. We watched the draw for the next round, and bloody hell!! Liverpool at home.

The following week we had Arsenal at home again. This time in the league. It was freezing and I was full of cold. I sat in the main stand as I felt unwell, freezing and shivering. I should have stayed at home being so sick, but I wanted to go and I went on my own. A lady in front of me took pity on me and gave me an oxo drink and a mars bar. The crowd shouted to Kenny Samson to shoot every time that he touched the ball, in reference to his own goal the week before. We took the lead in the second half and looked sure of the victory. However, two late Arsenal goals robbed us, and I trudged of home feeling awful.

It was the day of the cup tie with Liverpool and I was back in the Street End. This was a real cup tie, and it had some savage tackles flying around from both sides. Peter Eastoe gave us the lead early in the game and we all went nuts. The place exploded after sixty minutes when Imre Varadi knocked in a second. The roar was back and our neighbours were getting a good hiding from us. Liverpool refused to roll over and struck back with a Jimmy Case goal. This left us with a nail biting final fifteen minutes, but we held out and made it through. Celebration time!!

That win against Liverpool was probably the last real highlight of the season. We did make it to the quarter finals of the cup where we got stuffed by Man City. Our league form dipped and so did the crowd. The last few home games were very poorly attended, with many open spaces to be seen around the stadium. Surely next season would be better? After all the bad results, boos, throwing of seat covers onto the pitch, and low attendances, manager Gordon Lee was sacked. I liked Gordon and I still think it is unfair how he is slated by some people at times. For a couple of seasons he had us playing well.

The wonderful sight that is Goodison Park

It was time for someone else to take control, and in stepped a former club hero in the shape of Howard Kendall. It was also the time of many changes. I had left school and started a YOP or YTS, whatever it was called? Marty had moved away from the area I lived in and we hardly saw each other. Big Bobby Latchford, my first football hero had moved on and new players had started to appear on the team sheet. Adrian Heath, Kevin Richardson, Neville Southall, even Howard Kendall gave himself a few games.

This was a tough season. We had no luck in the cup competitions, but hard work in the league gave us a much better finish of 8th place. We were going in the right direction. In December of 1981 we played Swansea at home and won 3-1. Bob Latchford scored for them that day. This was the day that Kendall donned an Everton shirt and hit the pitch. It was fantastic to see him play, even if the team did have to slow down for him. His touch was still magic and it was a pleasure to see him grace the turf. He played the next few games as well, but it was all through the need of cover and once people were fit he stood back and let them in.

The 82/83 season started with a loss at Watford. Peter Reid and Kevin Sheedy had joined our ranks as we looked to build on last seasons improvements. We gave Villa and Spurs a thumping in our first two home games and I was feeling good. I was by now determined that I would attend an away game, and it finally happened on Saturday 25th September when we played Coventry City at Highfield Road. We got stonked 4-2 by them, but I had at last experienced an away fixture.

Plucky Newport were our opposition in the league cup. We saw them off over two legs 4-2, but the crowd at Goodison for the tie was tiny. Less than 9,000 attended the game, it was dismal. Then, it was a home game against our rivals Liverpool. My confidence was high for this one "we can do these" I kept thinking to myself. Ten minutes in and we were getting outplayed. Then, Ian Rush banged one in and the reds fans all went crazy. Glenn Keeley, playing his one and only game for Everton was sent off after bringing down Dalglish. We managed to make it in at half time trailing only by the single goal. The second half was a horror show, and still to this day I cannot believe that I stayed until the final whistle. Look, we got spanked 5-0 OK!! and, Rush scored four of them.

Arsenal then dumped us out of the league cup, before we finally gave someone a decent beating when winning 5-0 against Luton Town. In the new year our old friends Newport were back, this time in the FA cup. It took a replay for us to shake them off. I had still only attended one away game and longed for more. I soon made up ground going to the defeats at Villa and Sunderland, jeez!! I was the unlucky mascot at away games. An FA cup quarter final at Man Utd was next, would my luck come good in the cup? Nope!! we lost 1-0. Then, Nottingham Forest and a 2-0 defeat. I was getting annoyed by now at how long this losing run would go on for. Birmingham away was my last chance of stopping the rot that season. I went there full of hope and we lost 1-0. I can tell you something, I was almost ready to give up on away games there and then.

We finished the season in 7th place, probably because I was a curse to away games. The attendances had Goodison had shrunk to an all-time low. We were playing to a half empty stadium, even worse than that sometimes. It did not help that our neighbours were winning every trophy going either. I knew lads who had supported Everton for years who had changed over to the dark side and supported Liverpool. One thing I cannot stand is a turncoat glory hunter. Shame on them.

I was now 18 and earning enough to buy myself a season ticket for the Street End. Derek Mountfield, Alan Harper and Trevor Steven were now in the team. Our first two games were at home, winning against Stoke and losing to West Ham. Then, I was on my travels again, back to Coventry City for a 1-1 draw, hey!! at least it was not a defeat. I took in the boring 0-0 home draw against against West Brom, and noticed that the crowd was getting pathetic again. 15,000 turned up, it was a crying shame. Then. Disaster struck. My work was sending me to London for two months. For fucks sake, I had a season ticket. My mate was happy as he got to see the next few home games free of charge as I gave him the ticket until I returned. Then, I was off 'Darn sarf' for my stint in the big smoke. Well Penge actually.

On my first weekend in London we played Tottenham at White Hart Lane. I managed to get a ticket and watched us beat the spuds 2-1. Hooray!! an away victory at last. I also watched us lose to Arsenal and draw with West Ham in the league cup while I was down there. I made it back in in time for the home game versus Aston Villa in December which we drew 1-1. The crowds were by now getting stupid. 13,000 for some games. People were baying for Kendall's blood. They wanted him out and the board as well. The game against Coventry at Goodison on 31st December 1983 was as bad as it gets. That dire 0-0 draw was greeted with boos from the few that had bothered to turn up. We had scored just eleven league goals up to that point. Things looked bad as we sat near the foot of the table. Nobody, but nobody, could have foretold what was about to happen next.

January saw us record victories in the league and both cups. It was improving, but nobody was really expecting much. We started to win more games and progressed further in both cups. I took us three attempts to get past Gillingham in the FA cup, but with did it and something started to say "maybe! Just Maybe!". In February we played Aston Villa in the league cup semi-final, winning 2-0. 40,000 turned up that night, and while I was happy that a good crowd was there to get behind the players, I was still a bit miffed off that it had taken the chance of a trophy to get people back into the ground. We lost the second leg of the semi 1-0 at Villa, but we had done them 2-1 over the two legs. Everton were in a final, we were going to Wembley against our rivals Liverpool.

Apart from the derby, the home attendance continued to be low. We were winning a lot of games by now and I was stunned that it had not risen. Even the quarter final FA cup tie at home to Notts Country attracted less than 20,000. However, everyone was looking for a ticket for the league cup final and that really annoyed me.

The Upper Gwladys Street stand.

March 25th, Wembley stadium. We travelled by coach with an amazing atmosphere. The singing went on all the way to London. I loved it, an amazing experience. Some of those on board were already drunk when we set off, and the amount of beer that they loaded onto the coach was incredible. I never had a drink, I have never liked to have one if I travel anywhere. I am still the same now.

A sea of blue and red covered Wembley, inside and outside. The place was buzzing, pure electric, and then, something very special happened. Rivalries were put aside as the two sets of fans showed off their city "Merseyside! Merseyside! Merseyside!" rang out from both sets of supporters and rocked the foundations of the old stadium. Followed by the beautiful rendition of "Are you watching Manchester". It was a very special day to be a Scouser.

The game was fierce and very lively for a 0-0 draw after extra-time. Now, it was the players turn to do the city proud and they did not let us down. Both teams began a lap of honour of the stadium together. Many red and blue players walking together with their arms around each other shoulders as they applauded the fans. They then posed for a joint team photo together. It was wonderful to see it happen. The singing continued all the way home and into many of the cities nightclubs. A draw that day was a fitting outcome for the fans. Three days later at Maine Road, Graeme Souness destroyed my hope of a trophy as he hit the winner in the replay. I could not attend this night due to work commitments, but the pain of losing was awful. Still, not enough to ruin the memory of that great day at Wembley.

Two weeks later we were at Highbury for the FA cup semi-final with Southampton. Well the players and the fans were anyway, while I was stuck back in Liverpool at a wedding. The game had produced no goals at all, but with just under three minutes remaining of extra-time pint sized Adrian Heath popped up with the winner. We were going back to Wembley. Three days later Southampton trounced us in the league, but who cares.

In the league, 17,000 watched us beat Wolves at home, while 28,000 turned out for the draw with Man Utd. The final home game of the season was against QPR when just 20,000 attended to thank the lads for what had proved to be a good season, and to wish them good luck in the cup final. The scramble for a cup final ticket was crazy, and everyone seemed to be an Evertonian again. Was I miffed, you bet I friggin was.

Saturday 19th May 1984. The songs and the beer had all been loaded and the coach drove us down to Wembley. We were the favourites to win, but I was nervous. I could not bear the thought of losing two finals in one season. While the final against Liverpool had been a great day out and softened the blow of losing the cup, this one we just had to win or I would never get over it. Being among the Everton fans all singing their hearts out gave me a huge sense of pride. I am of course biased, but Evertonians really are the best fans in the world. However, my nerves were by now getting worse. I had convinced myself that we would lose.

The teams walked out to a fantastic reception and the game got under way, us against Elton John's Watford. My nerves just got more intense as the game went on. I was waiting for it all to go wrong and Watford to score. I just knew it was going to happen. And, then, disaster struck … I needed a wee. I tried to hold it in, but I had no chance and the urge became too much. Off I went into the stand to find a toilet. At last I was aiming at an urinal in relief. As I carried on I heard a rumble followed by a huge cheer. We had scored, and I had fucking missed it. As I walked back everyone was going nuts around me, and my mates all burst out laughing at me. Of course I was delighted and sang along with everyone else, but I had missed the goal.

Half time came and we were 1-0 up. Everyone went for a wee apart from me who stood there wondering what Sharpies go was like. I thought "We better score again" as the second half kicked off, and I did not have to wait long. Andy Gray jumped up and seemed to knock the ball the ball out of the goalkeepers hands and into the net with his head. It was 2-0 and total bedlam in that crowd. If I am honest it was bloody fantastic as we all jumped around in celebration. With minutes to go we knew that the cup was ours. That was an unbelievable time and experience that it is impossible to describe to someone who has not been through it. The songs continued, the whistle blew, and the party began.

I never really saw the cup that much as it was so manic in the crowd. In fact, I got a better view of it at the homecoming parade. But I had finally seen us win a trophy, and it felt good, really good. The coach trip back home was superb. It was one mass party of singing and drinking. The driver got a few bob in tips when we reached Liverpool as well. The city centre was full of bluenoses celebrating and those out drinking joined in as well. Even kopites were invited, and many joined in to wish us well. After all, our teams had swept the board in domestic trophies so we were all happy. I have no idea what clubs we went in as everywhere was full of blue and white. It was wonderful, just amazing. We found ourselves at a party in Wavertree that went on until the wee hours, until tiredness, and the beer, finally took its toll and I headed off with a few pals to look for a taxi. I slept well that night and woke up with an awful hangover, but it was well worth it.

The next season started with the charity shield fixture at Wembley against Liverpool. I never fancied going to this so I gave it a miss. That is probably the reason that Bruce Grobbelaar scored an own goal by throwing the ball into his own net and gave us the victory. Paul Bracewell and Pat Van den Hauwe were now part of the squad and my expectations were high for the season. Hopefully another trophy and an improvement on the 7th place league position that we had gained last period. However, Spurs ripped us apart at Goodison on the first day of the season, followed by a mid-week defeat at West Brom. With this kind of start nobody could have imagined just what the season would bring. If you had predicted it at that time, then you would have been laughed out of the city.

We then got better, and how. At first it was all still a bit dodgy, including a rather forgetful 1-0 aggregate score against UC Dublin in the first round of the cup winners cup. But then the wheels started moving, it clicked, and we just brushed the others aside.

Apart from Grimsby that is, as they knocked us out of the league cup. Six league wins on the trot put us up among the leaders. They included a victory at Anfield when Graeme sharp scored that cracker of a goal. We also beat Man Utd 5-0 at Goodison and Stoke 4-0. The goals were coming fast and Inter Bratislava were thumped in the cup winners cup. Things were looking very good indeed.

Where we stick those away fans

   At Goodison we beat Nott's Forest 5-0, Newcastle 4-0 and Watford 4-0. It was starting to look like we had a good chance of winning the league. Something that was unthinkable the previous August. We also cruised along in the FA cup as well as Europe where Fortuna Sittard fell victim to us. By April we were romping to the league title and had made it to the semi-final of the FA and cup winners cup's. This was getting exciting, in fact it was dreamland. Then, came Bayern Munich, and nothing could prepare us fans for what was going to happen.

This game was already being classed as the final with the press saying that whoever went through would lift the trophy. A bit unfair on the other two teams still in the cup really, but this was the big game as far as the press were concerned. The first leg in Germany resulted in a goalless draw. Then, it was back to Goodison on 24th April for the return leg. I swapped my scarf with a German lad that night. Another item that was destined to be flogged by my brother years later at a car boot sale, the idiot. The previous season we had experienced two domestic finals. Now, we had a chance to compete in a European one. The nerves and excitement were full-blown. The songs were sung louder than ever. The team was cheered, and everyone waited for our destiny to take hold. Then, Bayern scored. I was stunned and gutted at half-time with the Germans leading 1-0. They had that valuable away goal. We needed at least two goals now to win and this was Bayern Munich, they were a great side.

The crowd played its part and roared the lads on and they soon responded when Sharpie nodded one in three minutes after the break. Bayern held strong and the game ticked on. We needed to score and time was running out. A long throw-in into the box was missed by the keeper. It fell to Andy Gray who had a simple tap in. Boom!!! Goodison exploded. We were celebrating, but nervous still. One Bayern goal and we were out. Everton had been incredible during that second half and they carried on attacking. With four minutes to go Gray put Trevor Steven in and he calmly chipped the keeper to make it 3-1. I saw little after that as the Street End had gone into party mode. I still have no idea how long it took for the noise to die down and the crowd to disperse. It was all just pure joy and I lapped up every minute of it. I can still sense the feeling from that night. I mean, we destroyed them in those last 45 minutes, we were incredible. It really was one of our best performances ever.

Between the two legs of the cup winners cup we had beaten

Luton Town at Villa Park to reached the FA Cup final against Manchester United. Two finals reached again, this was crazy, and not long after on 6th May we beat QPR 2-0 at Goodison to become league champions. There was still five games to play in the league so we had done it in style. "hand it over Liverpool" rang out as the fans of the new champions praised their heroes. The trophy was presented to the team and they went on a lap of honour. The QPR fans gave our boys a fantastic reception when they passed in front of them. I think I walked home in a daze that day.

On Saturday 11th May I watched on TV as the tragedy unfolded at the Bradford City Valley Parade ground. A fire started from a cigarette butt and spread through the stand. 56 people lost their lives that day with many others injured. It was beyond belief that this could have happened. People were just out to enjoy a game of football.

Four days later Everton took on Rapid Vienna in the cup winners cup final in Rotterdam. I never went to any of the away games in Europe, and I missed the final as well. I just did not fancy the travel abroad and work the next day. I watched on TV in the pub as we ran out 3-1 winners to lift a European trophy. Then, on the following Saturday I was back on a coach to Wembley to see if we could win the treble in the FA cup final. The game ended 0-0. Extra-time was played and it was clear to see that the blues players were tired. Two finals in four days is some doing. They were holding out though. That is until ten minutes from the end when Norman Whiteside scored an absolute stunner of a goal to win the cup for Man Utd. It was gutting, but we still celebrated our team's success in other competitions on the way home.

We also still had three league games to fit in, and a homecoming parade. The lads brought the two trophies back for a tour of the city, but Granada TV thought it was much more important to focus on Man Utd's return with the FA cup..Bah!! Stuff them. My last time watching Everton play Live as a teenager was a home game against Liverpool. John Wark missed a penalty by a mile for the reds, before Paul Wilkinson banged in the winner for us. What a way to end my teenage years of watching Everton.

What a wonderful sight

It had been an amazing roller coaster for the past year. We had been hoping that Howard Kendall would leave and then he somehow turned it all around into this incredible success. How did he do it? Who knows? Some say the Oxford cup tie when he opened the dressing room window and let the sound of the Everton fans come in before saying "That is your team talk". Others point to the Birmingham game earlier than that when he is supposed to have told the players that they were on their last chance and assured them that if they did not perform he would drop them and play kids in the side. Whatever he did it worked. He managed to convince these players that they could do anything, and they did. I like most other Evertonians, remain thankful to Howie for what he brought to our club.

On 29th May 1985, Everton's rivals Liverpool played Juventus in the European cup final at the Heysel stadium in Brussels, Belgium. Crowd violence had caused a section of the Juventus fans backwards and the wall they went up against crumbled and fell. 39 people lost their lives that day, and incredibly the authorities made the match go ahead. After this event, English teams were banned from competing in European competitions for five years. I watched it all happen on TV. I sat in stunned silence as once again people died at a football match.

Some Everton fans claim we were robbed of our chance of winning the European cup by that ban. We were certainly removed from the competition so we could not challenge for it, but there is nothing to suggest that we would have won it, no matter how good we were. It happened, and that is that, and no English team would compete over the next few years.

It saddens me to hear people blaming Liverpool for our ban. It sickens me to hear people calling them murderers. A number of Juventus fans still hold anger towards Liverpool football club and I can understand that as it was their fans that suffered. However, and this is my own opinion, if anyone is looking for anyone to blame then blame EUFA. They allowed the game to be played in a stadium that clearly was not safe.

CHAPTER 5: DREAMLAND TO DISASTER

I had known in April that my work would be sending me to London in June for the best part of six months so I never bothered with the season ticket. We beat Man Utd 2-0 in the Charity Shield, but I never attended. The first game I did go to was Spurs away, where we won 1-0 with the goal scored by our new striker Gary Lineker. I also saw us lose away to QPR, West Ham, and Chelsea Bah!!. My first home game was not until Boxing day, when we beat Man Utd 3-1. We had also been entered in that stupid competition the 'Screen Sport super cup! We made it through to the final that incredibly was not played until the next season. If you must know the outcome we got a good hiding from Liverpool in it.

We now went on a great run. Making it through to another FA cup semi final and challenging Liverpool and West Ham for the title. We beat Sheffield Wednesday 2-1 in the semi-final to make it to our third FA cup final on the trot. In the league we held all the cards with just three games to go. A trip to relegation threatened Oxford looked a formality, but we lost 1-0. We had let Liverpool in and they finished the job with us two points behind in second. It felt as if we had thrown it away, but that's football.

Our neighbours were also our challengers in the FA cup final. This fixture had pissed me off big time as I could not get a ticket. I was mortified, and when I saw people who had hardly set foot inside Goodison with a ticket it really annoyed me. I was offered one at a stupid price, but I never have or nor ever will pay over the odds for a football match. I watched the game on TV and we started great, taking the lead early with a Lineker goal. The second half saw the reds fight back and bang three past us. I was well pissed off again, but glad I did not have that journey home.

Gary Lineker had scooted of to Spain after one season with us. New blood in the side was Dave Watson and Ian Snodin. We and the red half drew 1-1 in the Charity Shield at Wembley, I never went again. Everton and Liverpool took on the title challenge with Spurs trying to cling on to our coat tails. Liverpool knocked us out of the league cup, while Wimbledon were the team who finally put an end to our FA cup adventures. The title had been a good race, but in March we went on a seven game winning run and basically sowed up the league. A 1-0 win at Norwich gave us the silverware once more. Howie had done it again.

Cutting the grass

Howard Kendall left us for Spain and his old pal Colin Harvey stepped up to take control. We won the Charity Shield, again, beating Coventry 1-0, and no, I never went. Our league form dipped a little and we ended up finishing 4th. We knocked Liverpool out of the league cup, while they knocked us out of the FA cup. Our hope of another trophy was gone when Arsenal trounced us in the league cup semi final.

Tony Cottee and Stuart McCall joined our ranks for the 88/89 season, with the former scoring a hat-trick oh his debut against Newcastle. We struggled this season in the league and trailed in placed 8th. It was a bit of a sickener if I am honest, and worrying signs had begun to show in the team. A couple of the glory days team players had departed, and we just did not look like we could tear teams apart any more. We had progressed in our old favourite the FA cup, and had made it to the semi-final against Norwich City at Villa Park on Saturday 15th April. Liverpool were taking on Nottingham Forest at Hillsborough, so we could be on for another Merseyside final.

I did not go to the game. Instead, I helped a mate to fit a kitchen in his new house. We started early that morning and were flying through it by the time that kick-off came. The radio was on and we carried on working as we listened to the match. After about ten or 15 minutes, the commentator mentioned a delay in play at the other semi-final at Hillsborough. Saying that there had been a pitch invasion. "typical reds" I thought "no class at all". How wrong was I!!. In our game we scored after 26 minutes and went in at half-time by this score. The commentator had mentioned throughout the half that the reds match had not started. Even that it looked like it may be abandoned. It seemed a little strange for a pitch invasion to go on that long, and when the commentator at Hillsborough came onto the radio we started to realise why. He mentioned that there were people lying injured on the pitch and that the scene was total chaos. Something had happened in the Leppings Lane end of the ground that was hosting the Liverpool fans.

We decide to go to the pub along the road to see if we could find out any more news. As we walked in we were great by sullen faces all staring at the TV on the wall. The place was silent and we heard the commentator saying "Deaths". What!!! What was happening? Looking up at the TV I was greeted with a scene horror. The pitch was full of people who had spilled out from the Leppings Lane behind the goal. As you looked you saw it, people were lying on the grass with others trying to help them. Fans ran with advertising boards as makeshift stretchers. This was serious, very serious.

Time was lost on me after that and I have no real recollection of much that happened. Once it was confirmed that people had died the shock set in. I found myself praying for these people. These same people who I had gladly exchanged banter with for many years. Everywhere there was silence. The streets, the shops, the pubs. People were stunned, the city was in shock. Everton's game had carried on and they won through to the final. But, I never cared any more, nobody cared, it was no longer of any importance.

That evening we found ourselves in the Cunard pub that used to stand next to the old City Pets shop under St John's precinct. It was silent in there. Nobody said anything, people just gave each other those knowing looks. My pint was going flat. I had had it over an hour and hardly touched it. We all decided to go home and walked across town. The silence was everywhere. Nobody was in the mood for anything. The heart of the city had been broken that day. Back at home I turned on the local radio station. Soft music was being played along with messages of support and condolences.

That rag of a newspaper then printed its filthy headlines that accused the Liverpool fans of stealing from the dead, urinating on police who were helping the injured, and blaming them for everything that had happened. That was not what I and others had witnessed on the TV clips. It was a terrible thing to write and they cared little for the families of those who had died. It was shameful and disgusting behaviour from that utter rag.

Liverpool FC had opened their Anfield stadium to anyone who wanted to visit. We went along to lay flowers and were greeted by a sea of scarves, flags, football shirts and flowers that stretched out across the pitch from one end of the ground. It was one of the most moving sights that I have ever seen, and I have no shame in admitting that I shed a tear. I took off my Everton scarf and tied it to one of the barriers. This was sadness beyond belief.

Snow on the pitch

Liverpool FC cancelled their next few fixtures. The players and staff were attending the funerals of many of the victims of the disaster. Everton played the following Saturday at Tottenham and one spurs fan jumped out of the crowd to lay a wreath in front of

the Everton fans. That was a wonderful gesture of unity.
Liverpool's first competitive game was at Goodison for the Derby.
A 0-0 draw that was a great match fought with passion by both
sides. The game was played with the barred fencing removed. It
had been taken down straight after the events at Hillsborough.
Clubs had also been informed to make plans to alter their stadiums
to all-seater grounds. Liverpool then beat Forest in the rearranged
semi-final and booked their place to play Everton in the final.

Everton finished the season in 8th place, and then it was on to
Wembley. I never had a ticket for the final, but I never wanted on
either. I just kept thinking how could we win it? Surely the most
fitting outcome was a win for Liverpool to honour those who had
died in the semi-final. Many people believed that Everton would
roll over and let their neighbours win, but I am happy to say that
was not the case at all.

I watched it on TV with a few friends, a mixture of red and blue.
Liverpool scored very early in the game and kept that 1-0 lead
until the last minute. The game had been rather boring to watch,
but with sixty seconds to go it sprung into life, and it was the
substitutes from both sides who brought us the action. Stuart
McCall slid into a goalmouth scramble to draw Everton level and
send the game into extra-time. Anyone who had any thoughts that
Everton may not be committed to the game was treated to the
Everton players and staff going into crazy celebrations at the
equalizer.

On they went and the Liverpool sub Ian Rush put the reds ahead.
Then, Stuart McCall scored an absolute screamer of a goal for his
and Everton's second. Two minutes later Ian Rush had bagged his
brace as he sent Liverpool 3-2 into the lead. That is how it stayed
and Liverpool lifted the trophy. The two subs had both scored two
goals each in the final, I doubt that has ever happened before or
since. I was not upset by the defeat and was happy that my team

had given it a go. The following week Liverpool were pipped to the title by Arsenal at Anfield.

96 people lost their lives at or as a result of the events of Hillsborough. Men, women, and children. It was claimed that drunken ticket-less Liverpool fans had caused the disaster. This treatment of the fans, those who died, and their families, was nothing short of a disgrace and pure evil. The slander was concocted to steer the blame away from the police who had made huge errors on that fateful day. It later came out into the open that many police statements had been altered as they tried to hide their guilt.

In September 2012, the Hillsborough Independent Panel released its findings after almost three years of researching the documentation that had been presented to them. They found that no Liverpool fans were to blame for the disaster, and stated the main cause as 'lack of police control'. The original verdicts of 'accidental death' were overturned, and as this book is being written, the new inquests into the deaths of those who died at Hillsborough are ongoing. Hopefully they will get the justice that they so morally deserve.

A few years after the Hillsborough disaster I noticed a sign that read "I am an Evertonian, but on April 15th every year I support Liverpool". That summed it up for me and I have lived by that message on that sign ever since. They will never be forgotten.

CHAPTER 6: LOW AND HIGH IT IS

The new season came and we did not improve much. We went out of both cups and Liverpool beat us. We had some decent home results and Mike Newell banged in a few goals as we finished the league in 6th place. I had gone to the away game at Middlesbrough in the FA cup. A freezing day in January and a boring 0-0 result. On my way back to Liverpool I started wondering why I went to away games. The fun had gone and I decided to have a break from them.

To be honest it was not just the away matches. It was the home games as well. Don't get me wrong now, I still loved Everton with a passion, but something had changed and the excitement of going to a game was just not on the high-level that it had always been. I think it was the events at Hillsborough that had done it to me. Football lost some of its appeal that day, and I wondered if I would ever get it back.

We lost at Goodison 3-2 on the opening day of the 90/91 season. Big Nev did his half-time sit in this day. The results were not good and at the end of October manager Colin Harvey was sacked. Jimmy Gabrial took charge for one game before .. Oh my deary me, Howard Kendall returned. It was a bit of a shock, but it was Howie, our most successful ever manager, and he was welcomed back. The results improved a little and Howie steered them away from the relegation zone to a 9th place finish.

The boxing day fixture that season had been at home to Aston Villa. I never went. My son was having his first Christmas and I wanted to spend my time with him. In fact, I did not attend another home game until march when we drew with Nottingham

Forest. No away ground had the pleasure of my company. I was just not bothered with the travelling any more, and I wanted the time with my family.

The old Everton mosaic that was found in the Sandon pub

Any hopes of kendall bringing back the glory days were quickly dashed. The team finished 12th and 13th in the next two seasons in which I saw less than twenty home games in total. The season began in August 1993. We won three, then we lost three, then we won two, then we lost two. I had only been to four or fives home games by the time that Howie resigned in December of that year. Jimmy Gabrial took over until January and we recorded six defeats and a draw during that period. Next up was Mike Walker. Could he get us flying in the league? …. Nah!!

It was awful, just awful, and resulted in one of the biggest scares that Evertonians had ever experienced. Week by week we slipped closer to the relegation Zone, and we looked like a team heading for the drop. It all came down to the final match of the season against Wimbledon. If we lost we were down. A draw and we needed a miracle. Simply, we had to win. But being Everton we were never going to do anything straightforward.

May 7th 1994, our day of destiny. Everton had never been relegated in my lifetime, and if they were going down, then there was no way they were going to go through it without me. Plus, we needed to scream and cheer that stadium to its foundations. The outside of Goodison Park was heaving with people. The crowds were far too big to get everyone into the ground, but many people had just turned up as that is where they wanted to be. Unlike our neighbours, we are not a club who flashes flags and banners in our ground. However, today there were thousands of 'Good Luck Blues!' posters to be seen around the ground. The crowd was up for the occasion and roared on the team when they ran out onto the pitch. The Park End stand was still under construction and many workmen in hard hats could be seen watching the game. The stand also gave a few of those outside the opportunity of a free viewing as long as they were willing to scale up the trees in Stanley Park. Of course many did, and the sight of them up there just added to the buzz. This was it. Come on you blues!!!.

Anders Limpar. A good footballer, but what the fuck was he doing when he threw his arm up to handle in our area. The result, a penalty to Wimbledon. The outcome, 1-0 down. This was bad, but we still had most of the game to go. The comeback was made much harder on twenty minutes when Gary Ablett put the ball into his own goal. 2-0 down, and to be honest at that point I thought we were relegated. A few minutes later Limpar made up for his mistake earlier when treating us to his theatrical skills while diving in the box. The referee fell for it and I for one cared little about it being the wrong decision, this was survival. Up stepped Graham Stuart and calmly slotted the ball home. We still had a chance as we went in for half-time one goal behind.

The second half started and the nerves became worse. We could not get a sight on goal, and that clock was ticking away. It was looking bad for us, and with just twenty three minutes remaining we needed to find a way through. Then, up stepped Barry Horne. The ball fell to him near the centre circle. He took a touch to knock it to the right before unleashing a screamer of a shot that curled wickedly into the top corner of the Wimbledon goal. The place went crazy. Go on Barry you beauty. We were back level, but results elsewhere meant that we still needed that winning goal. It was bite the nails time.

The house painting celebrating 125 years

Limpar was racing up the wing throwing in crosses and trying to create chances. Time was against us and cruelly passed by so quickly. Ten minutes remained. We were just ten minutes away from being relegated. Then, Tony Cottee knocked the ball back to Graham Stuart who side-footed it towards goal from twenty yards out. It can still see it now, and I remember everything about the next few seconds as clear as day. The ball seemed to take a lifetime to get towards the goal. It bobbled on the ruts in the turf as it crept it way forward. The keeper was diving across and we held our breath and watched as it crept under his arm and rolled on in to rattle that net. BOOM!! The ground went absolutely crazy. It was utter madness in there as the celebrations took hold. A few people had made it onto the pitch and had to be removed before the game restarted. And, now, that clock appeared to be ticking ever so slowly.

It was now hit it anywhere, just keep the ball away from our goal. Some people had a radio and others kept looking towards them for news of scores elsewhere. As it stood we were safe as long as we held on to our win. With minutes to go the stewards along with a number of police officers began to form a line around the pitch. I thought "good luck with that one" as I watched them. You could clearly see the uneasiness in their faces as they were given the impossible job of stopping a pitch invasion. Then, we heard it, that wonderful peep of the final whistle. We were safe and ready to party. The security lines collapsed as the crowds ran onto the field. A few stewards seemed happy to just move aside on let them go on. As for me, another pitch invasion? I was more than happy to oblige and on I went. It was a fantastic day, a great feeling, and a superb celebration. However, I never wanted to go through it again.

The next season started and to be honest we were bloody awful. It took us until November to record our first win and we sat at the foot of the table. We were clearly going to be relegated unless something changed, and the first change was the sacking of Mike

Walker. Everton legend and a former number 9 hero of Goodison, Joe Royle, was brought in to try and stop the rot. One of his first decision as our new boss was to sign the on loan striker Duncan Ferguson. Royle's first game in charge was a home fixture against our local rivals Liverpool. Nice and easy eh!!. Everton took the game to them and looked a huge threat. Ferguson was playing his first full start for Everton and he repaid the belief of his manager when he rose to head home a corner. His celebration was something to behold, this guy was full of passion for the cause. The blues kept the pressure going and Paul Rideout knocked in a late second goal that gave Everton the points and lifted us off the foot of the table.

We won our next two league games as well, and started to pick up regular wins as we stove to drive clear of relegation. We were also on a FA cup run and had made it to the semi-finals where we faced Tottenham at Elland Road. The media was slobbering over a Man Utd v Spurs final and few thought that we had any chance of making it through. We, however, had other ideas. Taking a well-deserved 1-0 lead at half time before Graham Stuart tapped in a second ten minutes after the restart. We were heading for Wembley, but hold on! What's that. Spurs were awarded a pathetic penalty and Klinsmann banged it in. Then Spurs took control and looked on top as they search for the equaliser. We needed something or someone to help us regain control, and it came in the strangest way possible.

With just over twenty minutes left to play it was clear that Paul Rideout was walking wounded. Joe Royle told striker Daniel Amakachi to warm up while he gave Rideout five more minutes to shrug of the injury. Rideout was taken to the sidelines for treatment and signalled to the bench that he was OK to carry on. Amokachi, however, took the wave as his instruction to go on and walked onto the pitch. The official raised the board with the numbers and Amokachi was on having substituted himself. Royle was left standing in amazement, but would later comment of how great a mistake it was. Twelve minutes after coming on Amokachi headed home a cross to make it 3-1. In the last minute he tapped in Everton's fourth and could have had a hat-trick in injury time. His celebration after each goal was one of pure happiness that the Evertonians lapped up.

We had a crazy run of drawn games in the league, but we did enough to drag ourselves clear of relegation and finish in 15th place. A pleasing outcome after that awful start to the season. So, it was on to Wembley, and an FA cup against Manchester United. We were once again the underdogs, and the media had already decided that Man Utd would be the cup winners. I never had a ticket to the final as I never fancied the travel there and back. Like away games where I had lost my appeal to go to them any more. I was still only attending a handful of home games as I was either working or spending time with my wife and son at weekends. I was happy to follow the game on TV and was all set and excited for it on the day.

We played well and managed to stop the predicted united onslaught. After thirty minutes, Graham Stuart saw his shot bounce back off the crossbar and Paul Rideout leapt to nod the ball home. 1-0 to Everton. Duncan Ferguson had been injured before the final, but was sitting on the bench. They brought him on in the second half and he held the ball up well for us to give us some breathing space. The nerves became shredded at times, but we held on and claimed the victory. Dave Watson lifted the cup to thrill Evertonians everywhere. I was a very proud dad as I lifted my little boy up as we stood on Queens Drive. He got a good view of the cup and the players when it passed by us. Maybe he needed to be introduced to a game at Goodison?

CHAPTER 7: A SON TO THE FOLD

The 95/96 season saw us opening with the Charity Shield fixture at Wembley. I never went, but we beat Blackburn 1-0. We had signed Andrei Kanchelskis from Man Utd and he brought us a much needed excitement. Andrei was a fantastic player, up there with the best of them. His skill was amazing and his speed was just stunning. I was still not going to attend many home games, but I had decided that my boy should be exposed to the wonders of Goodison.

August 26th 1995, home to Southampton. Myself and my lad sat in the main stand. I bought him a bag of sweets and a programme. We won 2-0 and the little guy was chuffed to bits at his day out, even though he had been a bit confused at times. We bought chips on the way home. Another bluenose had been christened, great stuff!!

Man Utd had tried to change the agreement for the transfer of Kanchelskis. They claimed that Everton should pay the pay-on fee that was due to his former club Shaktar Donetsk, but Everton refused, and as far as they were concerned it was down to Utd to pay the bill. Andrei was not allowed to play until it was sorted out so he missed the first few games. On his third game for us he lined up at Goodison against Man Utd. Early in the first half Lee Sharpe took him out with a filthy and horrible tackle. Andrei had dislocated shoulder when he fell and spent some time on the sidelines. When he did return though, boy was he good. He scored sixteen goals for us that season, and considering he had missed almost half of it that was a pretty decent return.

Andrei was a first-class player and we had found ourselves a gem in him. In November he was to seal his place in our hearts when he nodded in one goal and sent in a thunderbolt strike for his second as we beat Liverpool 2-1 at Anfield. "Andrei is a Scouser" was a regular chant among the Evertonians. We finished 6th that season and things look like they could improve.

The Dixie Dean statue with tributes to Brian Labone

However, the next season brought a return to the slump. The defeats were too many, and in January of 1997 the club cashed in on Kanchelskis. It left people wondering about how the club was being run and what the long-term future was. I was still going to a few games and had taken my boy along a number of times to see his heroes. But things looked bleak as we entered a very uncertain period. In March I wrote a letter to Everton FC just for a joke. I offered my services as their new manager as I believed that Big Joe was fed up with the board. They wrote back and thanked me. They also explained that Joe was not leaving the club so the position was unavailable.

Behind the scenes the club was is turmoil. Joe Royle was at war with the chairman Peter Johnson due to the selling of our top player and the lack of funds made available for replacements. Transfer deadline day that year was on March 27th and Joe frantically worked to bring in two Norwegian players. The chairman had other ideas and refused to sanction the deals. Royle was left with no option but to resign. Who can blame him when he had no chance of being able to do his job.

My pen came out again and I sent off my second letter to Everton. I pointed out their previous reply and informed them that as the position was now available that I was willing to be interviewed. They never replied, so you all lost out on having me as the manager. I was going to play our kid who is boss, and fat Phil from the Sunday league pub team by our house. Phil was hard as nails so we missed out on the glory days with him. Dave Watson was given my job until the end of the season and we just about managed to stay up.

Deju Vu hit us once more when Howard Kendall returned for a third spell as manager. He had no chance with the chairman who seemed hell bent on ruining our team. We had it tough once gain and the results were poor. A draw on the final day of the season saved us from relegation by the skin of our teeth. This was getting too close for comfort. Howie could not work with a chairman who refused to compromise with him, and he resigned after that final game. Walter Smith was brought in to take charge of the team and we all wondered if he could possibly do anything with the chairman.

However, the worst event that past season was nothing to do with Everton. It was all down to Michael Bloody Owen!! that pint sized striker who had burst onto the scene for Liverpool. My boy had loved going to watch the blues and he loved big Duncan. But when Owen arrived it turned his head. My wife is a reds fan (I know! I know! But I love her) And as soon as she saw our son's head being turned she was in like a flash. Within no time she had kitted him out in that awful colour and he had been transformed to the dark side. Blooming turncoat. I was heartbroken, but that is life. Four times I took him to that den across the park to watch that bloody Michael Owen. The things we have to do for the love of our kids.

Walter Smith found the chairman a nightmare, and the turmoil all came to an incredible finale in that November of 1998. Everton played host to Newcastle United at Goodison park on the 23rd of November. The game was screened live on Sky TV and Everton gained a much needed 1-0 victory. The real talking points where going on behind the scenes, as the fans and manager watched the game. Newcastle had put in a bid for Duncan Ferguson and chairman Peter Johnson had accepted it. However, he had not informed Walter Smith and he sold Ferguson from under his nose. The deal was done before Smith came back in from the game. Smith was furious and made the chairman's dealings public knowledge. Ferguson had basically been forced to sign for Newcastle. The outcry among the fans was immense and the pressure was on Johnson. He resigned as chairman within a week. His shares in the club were bought out twelve months later.

A run of wins towards the end of that season dragged us clear of any danger. We were mid-table finishers a year later, before hovering just above the relegation zone again for the 2000/01 season. That term had seen the return of Duncan Ferguson who rejoined us from Newcastle. It was one of the few cheers that we had in a very dark and depressing period for the club. By March of 2002 we were out of the cups and only just in the league safety zone. The club sacked Walter Smith and looked for his new successor. It came in the shape of a young David Moyes, who pleased the fans in his first press conference by calling us 'The People's Club'. He won his first two games in charge and kept us in league safety.

The Dixie Dean plaque

Moyes steadied the ship during his first full season and took us to a 7th place finish. Kevin Campbell and Tomasz Radzinski were scoring us goals, and only four defeats in our last five league games stopped us qualifying for Europe. Sixteen year old Wayne Rooney had broken into the team and was sitting on the bench when we took on Arsenal at Goodison in October of that season. With ten minutes to go the score stood level at 1-1, and Rooney was introduced to the game. Arsenal were on an unbeaten league run of thirty games. As the seconds ticked away they looked secured of keeping that run going. That is until the kid Rooney received the ball in the final minute. He pulled the ball backwards out of the air and left the defenders stranded. Then, he nudged to the right and hit an unstoppable thirty yard curler into the top corner. Goodison exploded, Rooney became the youngest ever premier league goalscorer, and Arsenal's unbeaten run was over.

I was still only going to a few games, and my laddo was still a red. There was a lot more hope around as we started the 2003/04 season, but it fell way short of expectations and we finished just one place above safety. Disappointment was not the word, but on we go. By the start of the new season Wayne Rooney had been sold to Manchester United, and we were left to wonder just what might have been. Cahill and Arteta were now our play-makers as we set about trying to improve. But would we?

The first game was at home to Arsenal and we got thumped 4-1. Oh dear!!. But it improved and we had a decent run. We beat Liverpool and Man Utd at home, and by the last few weeks of the season we were in contention to grab 4th place in the league. What an improvement on 17th the year before, but could we hold on and do it? It looked unlikely as we stuttered during our last five games. Liverpool were hot on our heels trying to climb above us. We won just one of those last five matches and got slaughtered 7-0 at Arsenal. But we managed to hold on to 4th spot and finish above our neighbours. Champions league here we come..well, maybe not!!

Liverpool won the champions league and we were left wondering who would go into the competition as they had finished 5th in the league. It was decided that Everton would play a third round qualifier. The hardest team in draw was the Spanish side Villarreal, and of course we got them. We lost the first leg at home 2-1 and faced a daunting task in Spain to get back into the tie. It became worse when the Spaniards took the lead and left us with two goals to find. With twenty minutes to go Arteta scored a free-kick and we had a chance to get back into the game. With time almost up we had ourselves a corner. It swung in, big Dunc jumped, connected, and the ball flew into the net. Yeeeees!!!!!! Then, referee Pierluigi Collina, who was taking charge of his final game, blew his whistle for a foul. No goal? What? There was no foul. It stunk to high heaven and disgusted blues everywhere. The cheating git. We were out and then lost the EUFA cup play off. What a blow, fucking annoying really.

The upset had a knock-on for our season. We struggled and finished mid-table. However, my work had been given a contract and I was one of those sent to work on it. I was part of a maintenance team that was being sent to ... wait for it .... Goodison Park. Our role was to work in the ground on match days in case anything went wrong. To be honest we ended up helping the bars and lounges to move their stuff most of the time. Sometimes we were called in mid-week to fix or install things. It was not that exciting, but it had its perks. One thing we could do was watch the games as our work was done basically done by kick-off time. I had a radio in case I was needed, but I hardly ever got a call during a match. So, I had landed a job watching Everton, pretty cool. It did have one downside. We also had to cover Anfield. I never watched the games there, though sometimes I would watch for about fifteen minutes if they played a European team just to see what they were like. I did watch the England v Uruguay game there in 2006. We had that contract for three seasons and I was a very happy chappy.

I saw a lot of things working in the grounds, some real eye-openers. We would be given a few programmes from the previous game that we handed out to the kids that we knew. We hit on the idea of getting them signed as we were always going past the players car parks. I got to see who liked signing autographs and who never from both Everton and Liverpool. Each club had a couple of narks who would brush the waiting kids aside as if they were nothing. I will not name them, but I did think they were way out of order for it. I will, however, mention Joseph Yobo. I have never seen any player sign as many autographs as that man. He would spend ages signing away at every game and making sure that everyone had a signature. Nice guy, fair play to him.

Look at that grass, just perfect

One early Saturday morning we were at the ground when the striker James Beattie arrived. It was still hours until the other players came in, though James was there for a late fitness test. A small boy and his dad moved over to the barrier of the car park as they saw him. We then watched in absolute joy as Beattie made that little lads day (Probably his dads as well) by posing for a ton of photos with him. At one point he put the lad on his shoulders for a picture. Great stuff and wonderful to see a player interacting like that.

It also provided a few fun moments, such as when I scored the opening goal of the season in front of the Street End. An empty Street End mind, but who cares. There was no ball, so I made one out of newspaper. I then walked behind the goal, ran into the area, place down the paper ball, and banged it into the net. Yaaaay!!! the crowd roared, well my workmate did anyway. Sometimes I would come out of the Park End stand and pass through the Bullens Road end to get to a certain area. If I had to do it during a match, then it meant me going through the away fans. Twice, bloody twice, I was going through them when their team scored and they all went nuts. Once it was the Man Utd fans, so I was not happy at all being in the middle of their celebrations.

At one of the home games in early 2006, Bob Latchford had come along to sell copies of his book '30' The story of the 77/78 season when he scored the thirty league goals. Bob had a table set up for him in the marquee behind the Park End stand where he could sign copies of his book for the diners. Just before kick-off time, the guest in the marquee will move into the ground to watch the game and return after the match has finished. When the guests had left the marquee I went in, purchased the book, and took it over to Bob. He was about to start packing his things away, but he was more than happy to sign the book for me. I asked him to sign it to my dad as it was a present for him and Bob obliged.

Bob asked me to sit down and we chatted as he packed away. The game was live on the screen in the marquee, so we both kept glancing up to see the action. So to sum it up. I was sitting watching Everton with my childhood football hero as we chatted away, does it get any better? They say do not meet your heroes as they will disappoint you. After meeting Bob, I had so much more respect for the man. He is a pure gent, who is so easy going. For almost twenty minutes I chatted to Bob and he listened away as I told him how I used to scream out his name from the Street End. He smiled as I said it. Of course he had heard this a thousand times before from other fans, yet he never allowed that to ruin my story. I was going to save the book until fathers day as a present for dad, but something told me to give it to him straight away. He was delighted that Bob had signed it for him, and he read it all on the day that I gave it to him.

My dad had stopped going to the games many years before. He had a really bad knee (the one that stopped him playing for Everton) and he found it hard to sit in the seats at the ground. He loved Duncan Ferguson "A real striker" he would call him, though he had never seen him play live. The final game of the season was at home to West Brom on May 7th. It was to be Duncan's last game for the blues and we talked my dad into going. A number of family members went with him in the Upper Bullens stand. I was working, but kept popping up to see him and hear him moaning about the small seats ha ha. West Brom were 2-0 up just after half-time. Anichebe got us one back with five minutes to go before we were awarded a penalty in the final minute. Up stepped Duncan who spotted the ball to huge roars, stood back, shot, and missed!! Well the keeper saved it. Nooooooo!!! the ball rebounded and Duncan thumped it back in Yaaaaaaay!!! Fan-bloody-tastic. Duncan had scored in his final game and my dad was there watching. Dad enjoyed it, but moaned about those seats and stairs and how his knee hurt. Twenty three days later that beautiful man passed away.

A heartbroken family made funeral arrangements and set about sorting out his affairs. I was in his house with my aunt when a knock came on the door. Standing there was one of my dad's pals in tears. We brought him in and gave him a cup of tea. He asked us if it was OK for him to buy an Everton scarf to wear at the funeral. He was a reds fan and he had my dad had wound each other up something silly over their teams. We told him we would be more than happy for him to wear a scarf. I carried dad to Z-Cars on the saddest day of my life. We had booked a church social club for the guest after the service. Dad was a very popular guy and over 300 people attended. It all started very sombre as you can imagine. My cousin had made a CD full of Everton songs and asked the staff to play it. It started with Z-Cars, and as the first notes played the whole club stood up and burst into applause. It was a very moving and emotional moment. The songs then got people going and as dad was so fun loving this was what he would have wanted. His red mate was their dancing and singing to the Everton tunes while waving his scarf. Dad would have been looking down laughing at that.

The family had bought flowers shaped in the Everton crest and other sports that he loved. One was even in the shape of a pint of Lager. There were too many for the grave so we took the rest to Goodison and placed them on the Dixie Dean statue. The family, even the reds, all agreed to attend the first game of the following season for my dad. The game was against Watford and we won 2-1. To win was great, but the occasion was everything, and a few drinks were raised to dad afterwards.

CHAPTER 8: TO THIS DAY

The 2006/07 season started well with a few wins and points on the board. We played Liverpool at home on September 9th and I nearly ruined it for us. I was working in the ground and was asked to move a freezer from one of the stalls in the Park End to a bar in the Bullens. I loaded it onto a trolley and wheeled it over to the staff entrance in the corner underneath the stand. I swung the outside door open and pushed the trolley through. Then, I heard a gasp from those outside. I had gone into the area that the players come into the ground to from their car park area. Hearing the gasp I stopped and looked around the fridge, and there I saw him on the floor, Tim Cahill. Yes, I had knocked him over and everyone was staring at me in shock. Tim jumped up and said he was fine and shook my hand. Thank god he was such a good sport, and thank god he was not injured as he scored the first goal against the reds. Andy Johnson added a second before the break before he made it 3-0 in injury time at the end of the game.

At last we had given our rivals a good hiding, and it was celebrated in great style. At the next home game I saw Tim Cahill coming in through the car park and he pretended to jump in fright when he noticed me. It was a decent season for us and we ended with a 6th place finish in the league.

The next season we improved and finished in 5th place. In one league game at Goodison we gave Sunderland a 7-1 thumping. We made it to the semi-final of the league cup where we lost to Chelsea, and we played in the EUFA cup where we produced good displays to win against teams I had never heard of. Fiorentina finally knocked us out of that competition on penalties.

It was 5th position for us again the following year after another good performance in the league. We went out of the League and EUFA cups at the first hurdle, leaving just the FA cup as a chance for a trophy. Macclesfield were dispatched in round three, and our reward was an away fixture against Liverpool. We drew 1-1 and took them on in the replay at Goodison. The game ended 0-0 and went into extra-time. With two minutes remaining it was heading for a penalty shoot-out, until Dan Gosling popped up and struck the winner for us. The game had been shown live on TV, and those watching had no idea about the goal as the station had cut off before it was scored.

This sits on a stairway for one of the lounges

At the start of that season I had noticed that the cup final had been moved back to the end of May. The 30th of May was the date set for the cup to be decided. When I saw that date I knew that Everton were going to be in that final. That date was the date that my dad had died three years earlier and I was certain that we would contest for the trophy on that day. Aston Villa and Middlesbrough were beaten as our cup run took us to a semi-final at Wembley with Manchester United. The game finished 0-0 after extra-time, and it was on to penalties. We took the pressure well and won the shoot-out 4-2. We had made it to the cup final, just as I had known that we would.

We took on Chelsea in the final. Some of my family went to Wembley, but I never. I visited dads grave in the morning and watched the game on TV. After just twenty five seconds of the match gone, Louis Saha put us in the lead with a great strike. What a start. It was the fastest goal ever scored in an FA cup final. It had the Evertonians jumping for joy, but it was not to be our day. Chelsea levelled twenty minutes later, before grabbing the winner eighteen minutes from time.

By the start of the new season my works contract with the football clubs had ended. I reverted back to attending just a few home games. I was there and full of excitement for the opening day fixture with Arsenal. We had played well in the last few years and things looked bright. Hope was again in the air as the team ran onto the pitch. We lost 6-1!! Those unknown teams returned in the now renamed Europa league, and it gained us more experience with foreign opposition. The league and FA cups were both let downs and we went out early in both. Our league form was OK, with an 8th position finish.

The 10/11 season saw us end in 7th position. This had included a nice 2-0 home win over Liverpool. I did not attend any games until November as my wife was pregnant. Our boy had been born in September and I had kitted him out straight away in our beloved team's strip. I was not going to make a mistake with this one. Everton's first game after his birth was at home to Manchester United. We were losing 3-1 as the match went into injury time. I was listening to a radio and was gutted they had lost for my boys first game. Then, Cahill scored, then Arteta. 3-3, get in there. We even nearly nicked it with the final attack of the game.

Those steep seats of the Top Balcony

  2011/12 we finished 7th in the league again. It was steady stuff from us, but would we ever push it that little bit more. Sadly without big money backing us the answer was no. We again had a good FA cup run. Making it to the semi-final were we faced Liverpool. We lost 2-1 Bah!! Once again it was not to be. It was up to a 5th place finish the next season, but the cup games left a lot to be desired. Alex Ferguson left Manchester United and our manager David Moyes jumped when offered his job. Moyes took a lot of stick from the Evertonians for jumping ship, but who could blame him. He had done a decent job at Everton and made us regulars in the top 8 places. I liked him, even though he never seemed to have a plan B when things went wrong.

I was still happy as I thought the change in manager was probably needed by the time that Moyes left. Roberto Martinez was brought in as the new gaffer. That suave Spaniard and his brown shoes. What an impact he had as he steered us into a 5th place league finish. Of course it was always going to be hard to match that season and we drifted to 11th the next. Oh dear!! The Europa league was fun though, and we had some great results in it. Beating Wolfsburg 4-1 at home and 2-0 away, and Lille 3-0 at home. Young Boys received 3-1 and 4-1 defeats from us, before Dynamo Kiev gave us our own stuffing and knocked us out. The league and FA cups of that season just needed forgetting about as they were so awful.

This present season we have done OK from what has been a difficult start. The 3-1 defeat of Chelsea was a great buzz, and incredibly we are still in the league cup ha ha. A tie away to Middlesbrough in the last eight of the competition was our reward after knocking out Norwich on penalties. The Norwich game was awful, and to be fair they deserved to beat us. 1-1 after extra-time and the penalties began. From the Upper Bullens I booed and hissed the Canary players and cheered madly for our boys. We pulled it off and it was a great feeling. I like those cup games as the kids get in cheap and you can see the excitement in their faces. That excitement that I once had when my dad took me all those years ago.

We have a decent team now with some really good players. The club has stopped caving in to offers for our best players and we have managed to keep them with us. Martinez is doing a good job, though sometimes he stuns me with his decisions. We look good though, and our attack is pretty decent, as was highlighted when we knocked six past Sunderland in a recent game. Who knows, maybe a trophy will appear again for us? I would love another one. Of course I am selfish and want us to win things. But, I also remember the feeling from those glory years when I was a young man and would like some of our younger fans to experience it.

An Everton lift

The huge money involved has turned football stupid. Without a big backer a club has no chance of winning the league. Three or four teams dominate the league and even the Champions league is set up to keep them playing in it and earning even more money. It is all about money now and the wages the players are getting are unbelievable. It saddens me, it really does. The prices to watch a game have gone pretty expensive and a lot of people just cannot afford it any more. A lot of kids are missing out on games as it is too expensive for their parents to send them. I would not pay the price of a season ticket now and I still only attend around eight to ten games a season. I would not knock anyone who goes every game, fair play to them. It is all down to the individual at the end of the day.

A combination of the Hillsborough disaster and the founding of the Premier league made me fall out of love with football for a while. But, it is the game that I love and even if it is full of money I cannot stay away. It is over forty years since I first saw a game at Goodison and things have changed so much. I still think back to those joyful early days when I was at the ground hours before a game and the result did not ruin my day. Maybe it is my age chilling me out, but I appear to have come full circle when I attend a game now. I will not arrive early though, no way, I much prefer getting in just before kick-off. But I do enjoy the experience of a game a lot more now than I did a few years ago. I no longer panic about our result or others. Whatever will be. I love to hear what people shout during a match and we have many comedians at our games that leave me laughing. I treat it as a good day out, and that has made it more enjoyable to me.

A lot has changed since I first started going to Goodison. For a start the Park End stand where I first saw a game with dad has gone. So have the ABC boards that lined the pitch and gave us the half-time scores from elsewhere. The terraces and those horrible fences have long disappeared, along with those two giant square clocks that we used to stare at when we were winning or needed a goal. Those semi-circles that were built into the crowd behind each goal for the world cup games in 1966 are also now history. The ground has nearly moved twice as well. They wanted to put us at the Kings Dock, and even tried to turn us into a giant Tesco in Kirkby. I am glad we are still at Goodison and I hope we can develop the ground and stay there. It is full of history and I really like the old cow of a stadium. As I write we are once more among the rumours of a takeover. Our chairman Bill Kenwright is believed to be in ill health. If he sells so be it, his health is more important. We will still be Everton no matter who the owner is.

Last season I bought a ticket as close as I could to where I used to stand as a kid in the Street End. We won and it was a great atmosphere, but it was nothing like those days of scarves tied around the wrist, wearing Birmingham bags trouser and a lumber jacket. Then again, I am probably being a bit nostalgic and just reliving happy days in my mind.

Moyes is to blame for this

I still think back to those old days every time that I enter Goodison, and I always looked towards that former spec of mine with a smile. I can still see me and Marty being pulled out of the Park End and put into the Paddock. My eyes will go to the exact spot on the pitch that I dug my heel into to dig up the turf. I see the glory days and those near fatal relegation battles. I picture the Everton stars that I have witnessed playing for us, and of course some great players from the opposing teams who have faced us. The delights of beating them from across the park, and that horrible feeling of when they have done us. The days spent freezing and shivering as drips fell from my nose. Sitting in a less than half empty ground cursing everyone who had given up on us. Those memories flood back every single time that I take my seat for a game. I am not dead yet though, and I hope to make a lot more memories for years to come.

Would I do it all again? You had better believe it that I would. I would do it all a hundred times over. I love Everton, I love the history, the ground, the players, and the fans. For we are Everton, and we will be Everton forever. Alan Ball was right when he said "Once Everton has touched you nothing will be the same". COYB!!

The Gwladys Street where I would line up early as a boy

Just before I finished writing this book, Howard Kendall sadly passed away. His death has stunned not only the Everton family, but fans of other clubs as well. Liverpool fans have given Howie some wonderful praise and I thank them all for it. There are talks of tributes, statues, or a stand naming in Howard's honour. I am happy that something will be dedicated to him, but it is a bit like thirty years overdue. He was a fantastic player for the club, and as a manager he provided us with our most successful every period. I thank him so much, not only for the trophies, but for the wonderful memories that he gave me.

Sleep well Gaffer.

Printed in Great Britain
by Amazon